Acclaim for **Sapphire** *ana*

Black Wings & Blind Angels

SAPPHIRE

Black Wings & Blind Angels

Sapphire is the author of *American Dreams*, a collection of poems. Her novel, *Push*, won the Black Caucus of the American Library Association's First Novelist Award for 1997 and the Book-of-the-Month Club Stephen Crane Award for First Fiction. Sapphire lives in New York City.

Black Wings & Blind Angels

POEMS BY S A P P H I R E

Vintage Contemporaries

VINTAGE BOOKS

A DIVISION OF RANDOM HOUSE, INC.

NEW YORK

FIRST VINTAGE CONTEMPORARIES EDITION, SEPTEMBER 2000

Copyright © 1999 by Sapphire

Vintage is a registered trademark and Vintage Contemporaries
and colophon are trademarks of Random House, Inc.

Grateful acknowledgment is made to the editors of the following publications, in which
some of the poems in this book previously appeared:

BOMB: "Breaking Karma #5"
*Bombay Gin: Annual literary magazine of the Jack Kerouac
School of Disembodied Poetics*: "Breaking Karma #5"
JEJEUNE: America eats its young: "Under Water"
The New Fuck You: "humpty dumpty heart" and "Neverland"
Nobodaddies: "The Feminist Photographer"

Grateful acknowledgment is made to the following for permission to reprint previously published material:

Edward B. Marks Music Company: Excerpt from "God Bless the Child" by Billie Holiday and Arthur Herzog, Jr., copyright © 1941 by Edward B. Marks Music Company, copyright renewed. All rights reserved. Reprinted by permission of Edward B. Marks Music Company, c/o Carlin America, Inc.
Warner Bros. Publications U. S. Inc.: Excerpt from "I'll Play the Blues for You" by Jerry Beach, copyright © 1971 by East/Memphis Music and Rogan Publishing, copyright renewed. Copyright assigned to Irving Music Inc. (BMI); excerpt from "Let's Burn Down the Cornfield" by Randy Newman, copyright © 1975 by Unichappell Music Inc. (BMI). All rights reserved. Reprinted by permission of Warner Bros. Music Publications U. S. Inc., Miami, FL 33014.

The Library of Congress has cataloged the Knopf edition as follows:
Sapphire.
Black wings & blind angels : poems / by Sapphire. —1st ed.
p. cm.
ISBN 0-679-44630-3
1. Afro-American—lesbians—Poetry. 2. Afro-American women—Poetry. 3. Afro-Americans—Poetry. 4. Race relations—Poetry. I. Title II. Title: Black wings and blind angels.
PS3569.A63B58 1999 2000
811 .54—dc21 99-37238
CIP

Vintage ISBN: 0-679-76731-2

*Author photograph © Lina Pallotta
Book design by Virginia Tan*

www.vintagebooks.com

Printed in the United States of America
10 9 8 7 6 5 4 3

For the family I am creating

through friendship, truth, and love

Acknowledgments

I wish to thank and acknowledge the following institutions and people: Yaddo, Künstlerhaus Schloss Wiepersdorf, The Writers Room, and the professors and leaders of the writing workshops I attended at Brooklyn College as an M.F.A. student, where many of these poems were first written and "workshopped." Special thanks goes to my fellow writers in those workshops at Brooklyn College whose opinions, encouragement, and constructive criticism I look back on and draw on to this day. I also wish to extend thanks to my editor at Knopf, Victoria Wilson, and her assistant, Lee Buttala; and to my agent, Charlotte Sheedy, and her assistant, David Forrer. I also especially wish to acknowledge and offer my thanks to Amy Scholder for her help and guidance with this book. I also want to acknowledge the absolutely amazing support of my friends, fellow travelers on the road, Patricia Bell-Scott, Fran Gordon, Jayne Austin-Williams, and Brigdhe Mullins, who by reading parts of this manuscript, or by just being in my world, have helped and encouraged me to deal with the often difficult material of the text and my life.

What wound did ever heal but by degrees?

WILLIAM SHAKESPEARE

The giving up of personality traits, well-established patterns of behavior, ideologies, and even whole lifestyles . . . These are major forms of giving up that are required if one is to travel very far on the journey of life.

M. SCOTT PECK, M.D.

I dwell in possibility.

EMILY DICKINSON

Contents

Black Wings & Blind Angels

Breaking Karma #5

It is like a scene in a play.
His bald spot shines upward between dark tufts of hair.
We are sitting in a pool of light on the plastic
covered couch, Ernestine, his last live-in,
ended up with. But that is the end.

We are sitting in the beginning of our lives now
looking at our father upright in his black
reclining chair. It's four of us then, children,
new to Los Angeles—drugs, sex, Watts burning,
Aretha, Michael Jackson, the murder of King,
haven't happened yet.

He is explaining how things will be—
Which one will cook, which one will clean.
"Your mama," he announces, "is not coming."

Two thousand miles away in the yellow
linoleum light of her kitchen, my mother
is sitting in the easy tan-colored man's lap.
Kissing him. Her perfect legs golden like
whiskey, his white shirt rolled up arms that
surround her like the smell of cake baking.

"Forget about her," my father's voice drops like
a curtain, "she doesn't want you. She never did."

II

Holding the photograph by its serrated edges, staring,
I know the dark grey of her lips is "Jubilee Red"
her face brown silk. I start with the slick
corner of the photograph, put it in my mouth like it's
pizza or something. I close my eyes, chew, swallow.

Breaking Karma #6

I'm in the movies now playing the part
of the girl who broke my heart.
My mouth, strobe-light pink, bounces off blue sequins.
In the wings a white boy in a wheelchair moans,
"Oh operator please get straight."

SHE takes the stage now. Big yella gal.
Daddy was a wop. Mama was a nigger.
She's a singer. With a voice hot semi-liquid rock.
Her heels are hills, cobalt blue melting like   .
her dress into the firm breasts, fat hips & belly
of Black Los Angeles.

"Let's burn down the corn field," SHE wails.

It's 1968. Tito, Michael, Randy & Cato
are dancing down rows of rainbow colored corn
when a voice comes over the loud speaker:
There will be no ambulances tonight.   ˋ

"We'll make love, we'll make love while it burns,"
SHE screams like Howlin' Wolf, like Jay Hawkins,
like Hank Williams, like Van Gogh's windmill,
like the severed ear of black wind in a plate
of pigtails & pink beans,

like that bridge in Connecticut that collapsed
under the center of air shaking like
change in a cup.

SHE stands like the big legs of a nuclear plant
cracked at the base melting down a room full
of $3/hr assembly line workers who hear her
& shout, "Honey Hush!" & the crack in their
mother's back becomes a sidewalk, then a road
leading to a peach tree in "Georgy"
or a pear tree in Florida.

I'm eating popcorn & watching a Mexican
dump a drunk paraplegic BORN ON THE FOURTH OF JULY
in the desert his granddad rolled over
a century ago killing for gold.

At the side of the road an Okie girl,
selling peanuts & semiprecious gems,
hands me three pieces of black obsidian,
called "Apache Tears," the Okie girl drawls,
" 'cause after the cavalry massacred their men,
the Native women cried so hard
their tears turned black, then to stone."

Inside the theater the screen fills up
with a fat half breed burning, gasoline
in a blue dress. SHE picks up a
microphone & in a book she hasn't read yet
a white boy in a rented room puts
his eyes out with lye. "I rather!" SHE shouts.
"Tell it!" the audience shouts back. "Umm hmm,"
like the wind trapped in a slave castle SHE moans,
"I rather go blind," the screen melts white
drips down her face & disappears,
"than see you—"

Breaking Karma #7

You disappear down the hall
& reappear with a booklet
of fallopian tubes & belts.
You are thin like sorrow
with a shock of black hair,
43 years old.
I am 13,
beginning to bleed;
for 30 years
the ovum will drop
down the tube
blood like passion staining
everything—drawers,
the toilet's flush
bathroom
light bulbs
air between my legs
the fat cells
of my thighs
sucking
30 years
red opening
like a fish's eye.

I'm the age
you were when
you handed me that box.

I scoop my fingers
full of these last days
lick the blood off;
the red wanting of my mouth
torn open by the sound
of the rusty chains—creak, roll
as they lower your
sac of bitter light
into the ground.

"Ashes to—" I won't
say it. "Breast," I do
say.
"Stop playing," you snarl, "and *say* it!"
"Ashes to
cunt—"
"Would you stop that nonsense
and say it before
I slap your mouth out!"
"Ashes to ashes
dust to—"
"Go on!"
"No."

Fish
river
blood between our legs

filling a cup
sucking life out
a pen
dust to life
her to me.
My blood—
I release you to death:
the black circle of
a crow's wing—
the dark bleeding of
a dog's brain.
I release you
& step
out.

Breaking Karma #8

I

I haven't seen her in ten, eleven years,
I'm twenty-four, twenty-five years old.
My grandmother and aunt have heard I moved
to San Francisco. They call all the L's
in the book. The conversation is simple,
"Working where? Going to school where?
Chemistry?" Yeah, chemistry, I wanna be a doctor.
I remember them heavy, coffee-cream-
colored women. Doilies, food, church.
I don't remember passion or being loved.
There are hills in San Francisco, steep
stairways of cement, trolley cars, 1975.
"The city, is it nice there?"
Nice? How can I say "nice" doesn't describe
the way my blood gushes, how I bead my hair
with tiny red beads, hundreds of them—
beauty bleeding; I come to dance class
with red tap shoes and two white girls
come back with red ones too.
Yeah, it's nice here, I answer.
What do they want now, after the rubber
hose, the Tenderloin, tube down my nose
and throat. What do they want with me now?
What do I need a grandmother and an aunt
for now? After him, after my father? But I
am polite, launder my life, promise to call.

II

Why didn't I call, after all, I had
the number. Their tongues wag at me
as if I put myself on an airplane
at thirteen and said good-bye.
"Well, your mother tried to call," my
grandmother insists. "She did?" I counter.
"She sent letters," my grandmother asserts.
"I never got them." "Your father probably
tore them up." No, he tore us up. "No, he
would be at work when the mailman came. He,"
I don't like him but I can't let this pass,
"didn't tear up no letters. She never sent none."
"You never answered our letters or called."
No, I admit. Trolley cars here. For the first
time in my life I have enough to eat
and a room of my own. "Think you'll
be coming out here anytime soon?"
For what? "Uh sure."
"OK, well bye now. We love you."

III

My grandmother and aunt call again.
Awkward. "How are you?" *Church?*
How do I tell her who she knows is gone?
I do tell her, he beat me.
And I want to tell her, You slapped me,
twisted my ear, raged, but I don't
because it wasn't the same. He cast me
out. You, you found me.
My grandmother says, "I want you
to talk with someone," or did she say, "I
have someone here who wants to talk to you."
"Hello," the voice is thin, cold,
and in retrospect I will realize drunk.
"It's your mother," the voice says.
I realize she probably got handed
the same "I have someone here who
wants to talk to you" line that I got.
I chat on a moment about college,
my job at the phone company, say I'll write.
I can't feel nothing from her side
except sinking, it feels like a stone
sinking in endless water.
I tell her again I'll write, and
send her a picture. Because my sister
hates to take pictures and my brother
already is getting hard to find

I only have one picture of us together—
a color photo of three smiling
radiantly young people.

This time when they call I hear
the behind the scenes machinations,
"Violet!" a steel hiss from my grandmother.
The sound of the receiver dropping?
My aunt, "Someone wants to talk to you."
I wonder who. "Hi Mommy," I say.
"Sapphire?" she asks. No, it's Donald Duck.
"Yeah, it's me," then I remember! "Did you
get the letter?" I ask excited.
"Yes," she says, her voice sounds like
it's been ironed and frozen. But I don't stop.
"Did you get the picture?" I ask.
"Yes, yes," she assures me, "you look very nice
but who were those other two people?"
It's me now being laid out on some big
board being ironed and folded, frozen
to a small red speck that turns black
in my chest which is a box closing.
Breath. Where to find breath.
Putting the phone down everything seems
so still and coming apart at the same time
a box in my brain opens and the one
that's in my chest closes.

Breaking Karma #9

I am in Washington, D.C., at a Borders bookstore.
Me and the other authors have finished reading and are sitting signing
books. A young white girl comes up to me. She has a ring through her
lip and one through her nose, wild dirty "hippie" overalls, and kind
eyes. Kind kind eyes.

She thanks me for the reading and after I sign her book she hands me
a postcard book of beautiful African women and says that she wants to
give me a present. We both ooh and ahh as I flip through the book. She
points out one she wants to keep for herself, saying I can have any of
the others. The one she likes is of women dancing in a circle.

I choose a photo of a dark slender girl with African white teeth. Her
black body is photographed against a backdrop of sea. Blue like god.
So, a five by eight of the blue blue water and the upper body and head
of this African girl with tiny breasts, nipples like nodes of dark light
pointed toward god. She has a red pigment smeared over her jet black
shoulders. Around her neck are thirty or forty strands of red beads like
soft rings of passion rising. On top of her head, on a headdress of
black cloth shaped like a large donut, lies a huge black fish glistening
like a dark sliver of the moon, the upturned fins piercing the horizon
and the gentle azure sky.
> So a dark girl
>> with a bright
>>> smile
>> red smeared
>>> like blood or paint
>>>> over her.
>>> the blue blue sea the horizon the gentle
>>>> azure sky

and a fish
  a black
    fish
      on top her head.

I say black blood fish blue sea
  strange smile of a girl on
    the continent where our
      color tells us
        we come from.

I have only seen one picture of you as a child.
It is misty ancient photography. The face is foreign,
no recognizable feature or expression has survived you
to womanhood.
Your child-self crouches brown on a Philadelphia
porch in clothes from the first quarter of this century.
There is some type of nose-twitching mouse quality to you,
fear. A would-be beauty with no trace of the crooked
teeth, the veins in your hands, even the eyes that end up
so big, seem small and strange now.
What stays with me is how small, how very small, a child you are.
And how from a pile of photos of other children I would not
have been able to pick you out as mine,
and of course you are not mine.
You are the porch's
South Philadelphia's
the adults around you
the red brick

of a row
house.
You are colored in
the twenties.
You are the future's
but nobody knows
what that is.
I am who
will be born
to you
but you don't know that
sitting on the step
tiny toy of a child
you don't even know
where babies come from
or that you will
have to bleed every month
and break open
four times
for four different lives.
You are clasping
your knees
gazing past a camera
in a childhood that is gone
closed like
the camera's shutter.
All is black now
gone.
I gaze at the picture

of where we come from
women smiling black
with breasts like arrows,
strong teeth,
and fish on their heads.
An astrologer tells me you have
Neptune conjunct your sun,
a fish, the sea, so to
speak, on your head.

      Our story:
        me, you
            blood
            fish
            water
            mother
            daughter
              I accept the inevitable confusion
                the facts bring.
                  I want to accept defeat, despair
                    but I don't give up
                      I keep writing. I keep going.
              You are my life. My BELOVED.
                My hate filled mother
                    who spit me out like a fish bone
                I don't cry
                I stand in front of a postcard
                waves frozen
                time

the dead fish
the waves
            breaking like the question
why *whoosh whoosh*
                        why

She Asks About My Mother

In therapy she asks about my mother.
I tell her about the moment at the airport
four children, one mother in a skirt holding
a piece of tissue. Child by child we pass through
a turnstile to the plane. The last,
I turn and ask, "When are you coming?"

She says she doesn't know when she is coming.
I was thirteen, I would not see my mother
again until I was twenty-six. The last
time we are all together is 1963 at the airport,
even then, of course, our father is not there. She is through
with him. I walk in the kitchen and a man is holding

her. She is in his lap. Once she must have been holding
me like that, in her lap, me drinking her, her who is not coming,
who did not come, never came, who was through
being our mother.
Twenty-three years later we will assemble at train stations and
    airports
to pay our, as they say, our last

respects to a little woman, who by the last,
or in the end, was hard to respect. Holding
on to this weight, depression, in train stations, at the airport

I am afraid the person sent to meet me is not coming.
I was twenty-six when I went to find my mother.
In therapy I pass through

the turnstile again. I am through
running. At last
I am willing to look at this mother,
to look at my uterus holding
its hard tumors. It was me who was coming,
in a pink dress, ponytail, thirteen, alone at the airport

with my brothers and sister. My brother? At the airport,
did you notice him? Watch him pass through
you a second time? I told him you were not coming.
That's the last
you'll see of that boy. He will not prove good at holding
on; neither will you Mother.

The therapist, even the stranger in the airport, asks,
    "Where was your mother?"
It is hard to explain not coming, a mother being through or me
    holding
on to my uterus, swollen with these tumors, to the very last.

Ghosts

There are thirteen windows in this room.
I see the tops of trees and sky, my parents
run thru my mind; my father
scurrying like a mouse. My mother is sitting. Why have I come
here, and what do their ghosts
want with me. I know I'm not writing poetry

but trying to build a bridge back to poetry.
I will go home to a hot stuffy room.
I have lived with their ghosts.
The black haired mother, her parents
on her back. We had, all but one, come
to bury her twelve years ago. My father

died at seventy-five, a stroke, my father
myself? Or me, myself—where is poetry,
the feeling I used to have, will it come
in the middle of exercises? Finally I have a room
with windows. Finally my parents
are dead, are ghosts.

How they beat me, left me, laughed at me, are ghosts.
I see him frozen, hurrying, in a picture, my father.
I seldom saw my parents
together. My mother never mentioned my father's poetry.

I found it after he died. I was in his room
before his funeral. I had come

from New York to bury this father, come
to throw dirt on the recovered ghosts
of memory, willing to believe as I lay down in his room
I was a liar. Then my sister says, my father
got her while she was in diapers. In his poetry
he talks of sunsets and doesn't mention his parents.

My mother said he was ashamed of his parents.
When it is my time who will come?
I have no children except this poetry that isn't poetry.
Our father's penis is the ghost
we suck in our dreams. Still I miss that father,
raise him from photographs to come sit in my room.

Here at the writers' colony I attempt poetry in a room.
I see my mother and father at the top of the sky. My parents
have come here, home, to help me, ghosts.

False Memory Syndrome
(or, In the Dream)

In the dream my father
is a mean man
who is fucking with me up to the
time I am grown
He puts his big finger between
my legs and pushes   pushes hard
mean
in the dream my body is good
to me and doesn't let his horrible
finger in
In the dream I pass thru
the bedroom and pick up a pen
I want to write on the sheets
I get the letter "I"
"n"
then the pen
runs out of ink
In the dream I'm young
in the dream I don't think
suicide
in the dream there are no roaches
and I'm not all alone
In the dream I pass thru the room
a second time and find a two headed
rooster drawn on the wall
YO HO HO   YOU! YOU! is written
around the baseboards in red
in the dream I fold the wall and put it
in my pocket

in the dream
I get out
I am a smart girl and go on to college
in the dream I don't
kill myself and live a lonely life
in the dream I resist
He doesn't get in
and I fight back.

An Ordinary Evening

My sister tells me it was just an ordinary evening, but evening is never ordinary is it? Once the sun has started to climb down the sky things change. You and she were sitting in the den—the olive green vinyl couch, sports trophies, new color TV, pictures of Kennedy and King we keep turning to the wall, plate glass door, concrete steps to the back-yard. You were sitting in the den, by the tone of your voice you could have been asking are there any more hot dogs left or saying let's go get high. She said you just turned around and looked at her and said, "Let's kill him, let's kill the old man."

Blood on the Tracks
(or, I'm So Lonesome I Could Die)

train yards, uniforms
stations like flags
& steel bathrooms,
I ride close to the rail
with what I can carry
coffee light over the long grass
that is my country
rolling with that easy feeling
that dark pop top of light
fizzing like a razor blade
over the eyeballs of yellow
leaning out the direction
of nowhere backwards
rolling with the music
that is my time—loneliness
chrome flicker in the bright
boxes of ending briefly
& it was in the '70s I evolved
moved on up
& no longer thought
about killing everyday—
old people or babies
or somebody famous like John Lennon.
I understand why he had to die—
the damned Dakota
that Japanese bitch
all dressed in black,

all that dope, food, fame
studio time.
I dreamed, fantasized something as American
as credit cards & cancer
I fantasized shooting the famous
my wheels rolling fugitive
across the life
that is a train of losers
xeroxed back to back
plastic colored heavy water
wrapping around the axle of light
breaking like a bullet
through the greyhound
chemical smell
of the steel shit hole's
blue water in the black of the bus
registered like a holster
of discomfort slung
on the torn negligee of
dried grief.
& this old bitch
who we did the favor
of killing
doesn't have shit
to steal.
We don't want
silverware

or crystal
we don't want mahogany furniture
"Where's the money bitch!"
"She can't talk Pit Bull. She's dead."
The bottom of the vase is thick
crystal grapes
I break—
pull up
the old bitch's
nightgown
"What you gonna do, Spooky?"
It's 1962.
"Fuck this hoe up."
I jam her
wrinkled ass
with the glass dick.
It won't go in
but she bleeds
until 1992
words like
borderline psychopath
loser in blue jeans
green light off the Cape
of Dead Kennedys
white water
a bridge collapses
& I'm homeless

down to a screwdriver
& a dream
& the memory of Annette Funicello
in a white sweater
black skirt
& a Mouseketeer cap.
I know I'm stupid
I know I'm worthless
but I coulda been a star—
a stupid worthless star.
What I can't
be
I kill
turn to trains
to the man snoring
in the seat next to me:
WAKE UP motherfucker
& die!
I got a suitcase of hormones,
sparkle plenty & blond
love bones
& I want,
was born
to kill.
What I can't get over is:
we never had a chance
& now the dance is over

lying on its back
like a disemboweled dog
having seizures
in the crater of its
missing penis.
There's a full moon
on Main Street
& this pot of lye
is going in somebody's eyes.
Strawberry Fields
forever
          my ass
I hate you!
You see how Lana Turner
went down?
& that bitch that usta
play Kitty on Gunsmoke?
America does not
take care of its
own swimming pool
of packaged cheese
burgers broken
thigh bone
of a dog
eaten in the red
light of a train track
& if I had it to do all over

I would have murdered
my mother
& ate that bitch's heart
then rammed
a lamp up
her pussy
so the world
could see the
                 knife

                     cut

                         of a

                             tear
rolling through cattle yards
& remembered music,
I remember music
I couldn't make
& I want to
kill.

Lighthouse
(or, 6 a.m. the dream)

"6 a.m. the dream: at some halfway house.
No sympathy for the men. See grass, stone light-
house . . . 11:07 a.m. . . . could just be a biological urge
. . . or it could be a mechanism to avoid . . . feeling?
Also it felt like the scenario is basically one
of humiliation." I know I shouldn't have

coffee or sugar. It's Monday 5:45 p.m. and I have
had both. It's raining, I dream of my own house
one day. In many ways addiction has won
in my life. What is light?
Dark is the absence of light. I have a feeling
light is more. And the ur- urge

toward darkness, satiety, inertia—as much an urge
as the one I have
toward light! I have no feeling
sometimes I am dead, stone lighthouse
alone in water. Feeling is not light.
A tongue run up your torso can be one

kind of light? "Electromagnetic radiation . . ." *American Heritage,*
        number one.
". . . source of light . . ." Dark urge
pausing in the middle. Number two, perceiving light
I have
stopped, tried to live outside the house;
I offer myself to water feeling

dead, numb, depressed, and stupid. Feeling
as if I'll never feel again—one

reason, I don't enter the house
in the middle of the water's dark urge.
One reason I have
entered the electromagnetic radiation, light,

fugitive out the window. Light
fucked through feeling
until all I have
is one
ur- urge
to enter the house.

I find myself suffused with light halfway in the house,
the feeling like a sea of grass, green urge
root illumination, dark as blood, at last one.

Villanelle

At school the workshop focuses on villanelle
& sestina—the light at the end for counting
knowing, rhyming, European, white
I'm interested in the black howl,
light candles to invoke it.
I see where the cat has torn the bedclothes,
three layers apart with his claws.
It angers me.
Someone has a bed to sell for three hundred & fifty dollars
but it's a captain's bed. I been sleeping
on wood for so long
I want to feel the spring of things again.
As a child I had a pink bedspread.
I mis-write the "A" in spread, I made it
look like a "D."
Details of nothing consume my mind.
I rewrite word by word
jar sealed in fear
the soup spilled in my back.
Can a French form do anything for me?
Can the light dying behind my eyes be
recorded in rhymes schemes?
I meet this page in the morning beating back death
trying to re-member.
Vertebrae in my lumbar region blink like old neon
on its way out. The music loses me.
So many gone, so many pulled by the black motorcycle of death
I feel I am walking on top of the dead some days,
a black river of new shoes & feet cut off at the ankle
    & I see my father

I see my mother
I am their girl for sure
about that there is no question
I look for eyes in their faces
& see wet fire, dark light moving in waves
broken particles that form a valley. They know no songs
except the ones they had.
I see my brother.
He is dancing
in his black leather coat
before he stumbles & falls
& it gets taken from him
he is my brother
many things I saw him
do many times.
But dancing only once,
on Century Blvd
under pink lights
the gun stuck in
his tuxedo
Italian shoes
on a deserted six lane highway
acid white line
Hendrix orange velvet
breaking clouds
dark birds
on telephone wires
wings
& his feet
fluttering under a cloak of dark leather

do a dance I will not
see again until I see the Lakota
dance on TV
twenty years from the metal box
brain disease
walking in patent leather
back beyond CAMPBELL'S pork & beans
HANES undershirts & FROOT LOOPS swimming
in a bowl.

The park. I'll always remember
the way the wind pushed
the empty swings & the trees
were tall & quiet & we
were free there
under the silicone circle
of black light, the drugs
lifting us to a wild ecstasy
that was in us like
murder or motorcycles
& the candy cane moon
& the nigger dark growing
like the petals of pine cones,
the years, seeds
planted by the FBI.
But the hands that took us
would not be as exotic as the FBI or CIA
But hungry black hands that would
do anything for a dollar.
Money, though we denied it,

it was everything wasn't it?
A girl takes my tongue, signs her name
& asks me how do I like it?
I look at the empty swing
dangling over her death & realize
we don't know
we just don't know
whether the shoe drops in the morning
or an astronaut wears it to the moon.

Gently I enter this broken rectum of light
a silver motorcycle on black wings.

Sestina

Last night after school I finally got around
to looking at the formula for a sestina
& thought of Crazy Horse dancing in the desert
& I asked, Is god gonna appear here?
I want god
         a blue light so dark
it stains everything for centuries
radiative hallucinatory rood smelling
like urine & frankincense.
One hip has always been higher
one breast longer
& my thighs & belly at midlife,
like stupid teenagers
are totally out of control
like Billie
& Bessie or diamond black Big Maybelle
bawdy ballad red
dirt
rooster
throat cut in the sign of the cross
sodomized with a black cat bone
full moon
crossed with lye
road sign turned around
early death
gun shot
untreated
TB
HIV
roach wings floating

in the semi circular canal
(a white boy in the workshop, hip downtown grunge, shaves his
prematurely bald head, tattoos [you know, the whole bit], wonders
aloud if roaches get in poor people's ears when they sleep)
A girl says, Yeah, yeah they do, running like roads
out of nowhere, out of lines, & I fall back twenty-five years
before most of them were born & I whisper to Chris:
It didn't make any difference which side of the line you were on,
did it? When the wheel hit that dip & the motorcycle flipped
in the air in the light of a cervical vertebra
snapped in *infinitum* electrons spinning like wheels
around a dying nucleus of light scurrying
under cracks in some linoleum in Queens
& sometimes under the concrete the city is walking on
I see the cotton fields my daddy ran away from;
& his face, the love pulls me like an eclipse
to the worn envelope of poems I found in his drawer
when he died—
lines crossed in gasoline, burning.
& you know those ol' niggers back then
had about as much a chance of making it
as butterflies at Auschwitz.
Is that why he did it?

Now time is a light dimming as it burns brighter
turning me toward the dark then the light again. I hope.

Going Home

I am going home tomorrow.
Outside my window I can see trees
and through the trees I see the lights
of cars moving along the highway
as I will be moving.
I want to repeat window six times; windows—

Just now I ate a pear, it's in my mouth with windows
Windows and it's morning and tomorrow
is still dark but I see myself moving.
In the I Ching, Hexagram 46, Sheng, you see a tree
pushing upward and I see a car on the highway,
mine, me driving, the lights

pushing through the night. Lights
and the idea of windows
the feeling of moving along a highway
going somewhere. Life is today not tomorrow
depression does something to trees
or the way you see them. I try to keep moving.

As a military family we were always moving.
My mother adamant about Easter eggs and Christmas tree lights.
In school I learn about a Johnny Appleseed who planted trees.
I think of Kirk with thirteen children, wonder about windows
and that for so long I had none, and where I'll be tomorrow.
If someone doesn't drive should you use the highway

as a metaphor for life? Oh highway
of road kills, crashes, uncontrollable movings

of others. No matter how carefully you plan tomorrow
you could go to touch the switch and have the lights
not come on, a heart's blackout, anxiety running to the window
to look at what's left of Johnny Appleseed, the trees

lost to sight forever. But now I see the trees,
hear the low roar of the highway
and there are eight windows
in this room. And I will, am, moving,
Heliconian like, upward, my body full of lights,
switches, synapses forwarding me to tomorrow.

I see the windows, and trees, and tomorrow
I'll feel the loneliness of the highway, car lights
in the daylight. But right now I'm trees and windows, moving.

humpty dumpty heart

my heart leaks knowing
since you shot my sheets
with light,
lifting me out my skin
past sky.

i look for your tongue in light
& listen to tales of a new daughter
apartments, mortgages, wife;
knowing i was just a blurred night—
black, whited-out & lost.

out the blue you call back the years
like a movie reel rewinding,
after six deaf years i hear
you want to come over.

the silence of blind rooms
goads me to balance
humpty dumpty like
one more time the weight of light.

& i would,
but for the bleeding yolk
that lies in cracked knowing—
once it's eaten
it's over.

Under Water

xxxxxxxxxxxxxxxx
xxxxxxxxxxxxxxxxxx
xxxxxxxxxxxxxxxxxxxx
xxxxxxxxxxxxxxxxxxxxxxxxxxxx
xxxxxxxxxxxxxxxxxxxxxxx
xxxxxxxxxxxxxxxx
xxxxxxxxxxxxxxxxxxxxxxx
xxxxxxx
xxxxxxxxxxxxxxxxxxxxx
xxxxxxxxxxxxxxxxxxxxxxxxxx
xxxxxxxxxxxxxxxx
xxxxxxxxxxxxxxxxxxxxxxxxxxxxx
xxxxxxxxxxxx
xxxxxxx
xxxxxxx
xxxxxxxxx
xxxxxxx
xxxxxxx
experience
xxxxxxx
xxxxxxxx
the voice
life
ceiling
coming
down
for a while
the sunlight
shone

through
the window
& the ceiling
was luminous
with light
reflecting
downward
on the
xxxxxxxxxxxxxx
xxxxxx
xxxxxxxxxxxxxx
xxxxxx
xxxxxxxxx
devoid of tension
xxxxxxxxxxxxxx
chicken wings come
to mind
the plucked quality of
life that ensues
the pain
xxxxxxxxxxxx
xxxxxxxxxxxx
xxxxxxxxxxxxx
the light
that blinds
the sound like Hiroshima
but you are too
insignificant
to be so counted

but there are similarities
between
you and the woman
whose dress melts
on her body, disappears
rather, except for its
paisley pattern
left forever
from
her neck
to knees
imprinted in
her skin, the
yellow-white
shock of young skin
that she
had
no more
a door
a window
the sun
the steps
he led me up the
absolute
black silence
of light
never remembered
or understood
pushed back
into the bone's

caverns
lacuna
beam
flash forwarded
the amputated
arm
always bleeding
into photographs
of the past
smiling
as the people cheat
lie to you
xxxxxxxxxxxxxxx
freedom
a stamp
you grow
bitter
vomit yourself
up
it is the personal
property of a poem
bleeding
in the safe sorry of
xxxxxx
xxxxxxxxxxxxx
xxxxx
wall
to wall
that stretches
back to slavery

you are
the bent spoon
of a broken
promise
you are the one
who can't forget
but doesn't
remember.

I'll Play the Blues for You

It is more like a wolf
than a feeling. Yesterday it eats
at me.
"Loneliness is a very hard thing to bear,
but you can't let it get the best of you,"
that from Albert King's "I'll Play the Blues for You." "Loneliness

is a very bad thing, but you can't let it get—" Loneliness
You're out walking, or inside, and it, the wolf,
goes to bring you down. It hates you,
you think. Loneliness eats
too much, gives up easy, can't bear
light, becomes a way of life. Cloaks me.

Swathes me. The fantasy of him and me
fell through, was exposed as middle-aged loneliness,
absurdity. But I was laid bare,
devastated. I'd felt I'd escaped the wolf
at last. Like a caterpillar eats
the leaf, I would devour you,

spin a cocoon, and fly out someone you
wanted. The plan foils with me, you didn't want me.
My body is weird, a shock, the wolf that eats,
past perfect has eaten. There is a trap—like loneliness;
the hunter puts a razor in the salt lick, the wolf
licks and licks its life away, red blood bared

on the white snow. The way I was bare
on top of you thinking, Oh no! And I don't know who you

wanted, but you got a dying wolf,
it was not even me,
but the ur- refinement of loneliness
the sum of, the product eats,

lies, raised on fantasy, termites of eats
a mind laid open, its functionings bare
as that song Fontella Bass sang in the sixties, loneliness
standing up screaming, "Rescue Me!" and you,
wanting someone whole and passionate, get me
walking across the tundra, dragging the dead wolf.

I bear the dead wolf,
eat its liver, loneliness dripping from me,
drops of blood in the snow remind me of you.

The Feminist Photographer
(or, Camera Obscura)

The smell of sweat & leather climb up my nose as I
mount the splintered stairs in blue jeans & cowboy boots.
I've never seen another woman in this gym,

asylum for black men, boxers, glistening brown tan ebony
skins I peel back for a closer look at bad teeth & cauliflower
ears rotting in single room occupancy. I zoom in
on shiny black tits, chests wide like land & thighs
big around as my fucking torso. All that power & no money
no camera. Some of 'em can't even read.

These guys don't mind me taking their picture. They like me.
When they see me, they say, "Hey Erica."
I trap discontent's greasy meat in photographs
I blow up & attach to huge placards that hang like
dark pendulous lips on the marmoreal faces of museum walls.

"Hey Erica," he makes a lewd gesture with his tongue, "when
you gonna let me take a picture of *you*?"
The gym turns to laughter, my cheeks burn red.
I look at his big black body cut to perfection, his face smashed
flat & so ugly it's beautiful. I raise my camera, fix him in my

sight, then his hand drops down, he exposes himself & starts
to masturbate slowly, his pupils narrowing light as he focuses
in on the camera's dark eye. I press the shutter down,

command my feet to *move* but they don't & I'm trapped
with him inside this thousand dollar black box & I'm ten again

moving down the white washed steps to the basement
into the den's damp smell of cement & leather furniture.
Papa sits under the hot blue light of the projector
I can't see what he's looking at. There is no sound.
"Erica." Papa's voice drops over me like a slimy net.

"Come here," he commands. My legs, little pink, hard as
lollipops, propel me forward. Outside his pants like a rubber
duck in the bath Papa's penis bobs in the light. I turn
to run but am seized by hundreds of naked bodies on the screen
huddled in a large gymnasium, shaved heads glowing—

radioactive alabaster stones that roll
frame by frame till they come to a man strapped down
with no sound screaming on a metal table where his intestines
are being wound like thread around a huge spool. The smell

of leather engulfs me as Papa pushes me down into the ever-
lasting black center of silence, his eyes conjoined with the
        screen,
as he rams his penis into me again & again, finally
covering me with the sweet sticky stuff of life.

The Grey Wolf

The dew feels like wet bugs crawling over my feet. The dark is receding into dawn and an electric feeling like fear but not fear passes through me causing sweat to run in rivulets from my armpits as I stare across the field at the large grey wolf passing through the dew-studded grass at the foot of the black hills. I had always heard that they are afraid of people, that to come down from the hills they must be sick or old or injured. It looked like it had a knife for a soul, like its urine smelled worse than ten mountain lions', like it would carry off a small child in daylight from a game of ring shout. It, the wolf, did not look afraid.

I turned to the cabin. It was light enough to see the reddish soil I had grown up thinking was tinged with God's blood, "blood" that I now know is oxidized hematite. I look back at Mary Alice sitting on the porch. Every morning she seems to appear like some ghost while I'm out, barefoot in the grass despite snakes and being sixty-five years old, staring at the sun creep over the hills. The first time I see her each day I think the same thing.

I know her appearance on the porch is not mystical—she lays there in bed, like she has for years, pretending she's asleep. And when I'm out the door, walking toward the clearing or on the porch if the weather is bad, she crawls out of bed. I look at her long white braids, her worn faded overalls. It's hot, so all she has on is the overalls, no shoes, shirt, drawers. I think what I always think first time I see her mornings—we haven't had sex in fifteen years. I flinch remembering her hand over the years turning to a fly swatter batting at me. Remember the passion of her drying slowly like a tree stump, the only life in her seeming to be the cancer the doctors say is growing, running a produce farm in her bowels. I feel the light expanding across the sky, the accompanying warmth. I don't know what's different about today, maybe the wolf down from the hills, the understanding of being old, prey, limited, all abstractions that feel concrete under the light expanding across the sky.

I own the cabin, the land. Her father left the land and everything on it to her. She lost it in a crap game forty-three years ago to old, at that time, fast, Stinky Burkes; and ended up marrying Stinky to get her land back. But I had bought the house land everything one night to help him out of a gambling fix. Somebody was gonna kill his stupid ass. But he ran instead of paying the guy. All that's a long time ago. Mary Alice and I were in love then, I guess. We had whiskey, the moon, a big bed. Two women alone in the country. But that's past like when the wolf was in the mountains.

We make enough renting out the cabins, and the big house. Rent the cabins to summer people and the big house which you can't even see from here on the porch to a couple of young women who rent year round and use it as a bed and breakfast place. It's all beautiful land and we rent cheap. There's a stream but no lake. Summer people love lakes and since we ain't on it we rent for half what the Thomases down the road on the lakefront do. But they don't, the way it's set up, don't nobody own the actual lake, so our folks can walk down to the lake, swim and all.

We had started going together way 'fore I bought the house. Her tongue used to turn to blood in my mouth, we used to melt inside each other like butter or ice at high noon. We met each other at a dance with our husbands. Mine didn't last near as long as hers. I don't know why I never gave her back her property. I guess 'cause I bought it making it mine. Or because in those days she was liable to put some perfume on and disappear down the road and not come back with nothing but her life. She had lost everything once hadn't she. But I would give it back to her now. What difference does it make who owns what, we both old. I mean neither of us is ancient. She's seventy, I'm sixty-five. I could live to be ninety then again I could go tomorrow.

She knows she still excites me naked in her overalls, the faint smell from her cunt like fresh killed fish, her roseate tipped breasts hanging down like cow udders. The feel of her skin is a memory now. I replay the taste, the feel of her. She's poured water into the electric coffee maker, I admit I like some of these gadgets. I break off a piece of cornbread left in the pan from last night. I love the smell of coffee, the feel of cornbread crumbling yellow in my hand.

I look out the kitchen window at her sitting on the porch. The disease, I admit for the first time, is gonna win. I guess that's the way of disease, eventually. Like water, wind moving soil. You can do this that—plant contours instead of straight rows, alternate corn with alfalfa—but sometimes no matter what you do the wind and water and the soil creeps, slides eventually, away, to somewhere else. Erosion, movement of soil from one place to another by wind water. It's natural. I used to love her. I used to put one hand on her belly, push down and drive my other hand up her, my whole hand stretched out turning to a fist slowly in her vaginal canal. My arm slippery with Vaseline when we had it, bacon grease when we didn't. She always hated it. But she clung to me. I owned everything, was the man I guess.

I look at her on the porch now, the overalls spread over her body that's spread out itself over the years like a pink white fan. But she's not pink, white, only her skin is colored like that. We're both colored. You have to look twice but you can tell it 'less you're stupid or blind. We don't have no preference for each other based on our color. That's stupid. It's just how it worked out. Maybe we just knew it would be good for us to be together up here in this ain't nothing really but the Northern Branch of the Ku Klux Klan. We're kinda safe together, being black, looking white or "other," less like targets. Anyway what would we have done in the city? Been stuck in some ghetto?

Why am I thinking so much about the past when it's over and I usually don't get hung up on how things was; to me things just is, usually that is. I close my eyes, the coffee smell goes up my nose. I see the wolf now. Smell it. I'm in a cave surrounded by fur and feces and damp dog smell. I grab his slick luminous pink doggy penis. His teeth sink into the crepe-like skin of my neck.

I open my eyes remember something I read a long time ago in *National Geographic* about an Indian wolf trap. Where the Indians put a razor in a salt lick and when the killer wolf came with its hunger for salt and licked, each lick would lacerate its tongue. But for some reason the wolf would keep licking till its tongue was ribbons and its life was dripping out red on the frozen white tundra.

I look, my coffee cup is empty. I pour another cup knowing after it I'll need to pee continually for the next couple of hours precluding a walk or even a drive to town. I look at Mary Alice still seated on the porch. Then the vision of the grey wolf stalking the hills chokes my brain sending a torrent of blood out of my nose that explodes like the colors in the morning sunrise turning into a thousand little clots that begin to arrest the light in my brain. I'm thinking, I own everything, when the last light goes out.

Gorilla in the Midst #7

"Now," the nurse says, "the self-contained penile implants come in two versions: nonfluid mechanical and fluid, you know, wet and dry." She pauses then continues in her relate-to-the-patient-in-terms-they-can-understand tone, "The doctor can explain in more detail if you need him to but basically," she points to a chart on the wall, "the nonfluid mechanical, the dry one, contains a series of cup-like units operated by wires and springs." She raises the pointer to the chart again. He feels like beating her to death. "The wet one, the fluid mechanical one, has two cylinders filled with a saline solution that are placed in the penis. For the penis to engorge," she looks at him, "you know, get hard." She moves the pointer down the chart. "You press here." He averts his eyes from her stupid baboon face. He has to admit she looks like Donna Summer in a nurse costume, but if Donna Summer wasn't a baboon what was she? He sighs, "Maybe." "Huh?" she responds making him realize he's spoken aloud. "You know vitamins—" "You do," she interrupts him in her coping-with-the-patient-in-denial tone, "I mean the doctor did tell you the damage to the blood vessels that supply blood to your penis is irreversible?" "Psychotherapy?" he floats the question past her. "Well, it isn't really, I mean you don't have a mental problem." She shifts uncomfortably on the high stool, why her, why'd she have to do this shit? She looks away from him, points to the wall chart again. "This," she gushes, "is our state-of-the-art device, the fully inflatable penile implant. A fluid reservoir is surgically placed in the abdomen, two inflatable cylinders are placed in the shaft of the penis, while a pump-and-deflate mechanism is placed in the scrotum. The degree of inflation, and that is the wonderful part, is controlled by squeezing the pump allowing you to produce an erection that looks and feels normal. It's more expensive," she continues matter-of-factly, "and the surgical procedure is more complicated and therefore somewhat riskier. But there's risk in getting a tooth pulled. Look honey," she leans forward assuming a conspiratorial tone of camaraderie that she wouldn't have if she'd looked into his eyes, "if you gotta go plastic, as far as dick, this is it!"

Gorilla in the Midst #8

Dreaming it reminded him of those
favors at birthday parties
when he was a kid—
curled up pink and blue paper,
plastic snout you blew thru
till it inflated and unfurled
whee!
brittle pink paper
flat to full
only this was his dick
the life of the party
between his legs
squeeze pump expand
party time
bigger
taut
unfurl
blue
whee!
he's blowing—
the spikes of crepe paper at the
end of the favor
stand up in the wind
it's all pink
and hard
now
Where is she?

Gorilla in the Midst #9

The wheels of the car are rolling
unfurling like black flags in the sun
the street's a beat
thru Hades
he's gone
black and white
Lucky Strike
Let's shoot a nigger tonight
Manny laughs, he laughs
Manny Johnny
Did you really?
Yeah really shit?
We own this mother, he said,
casting his eyes on the street
mother
sun
wheels
night
everything wrapped
in light
he can feel it
in his throat
a world being built
full of nuclear lights
that ring like
telephones behind
his eyes
the night
is magic
like boyhood

he has it all
it feels like the five times
he did it
in twenty years
I'm not getting
no fucking operation
whaddaya think
I yam
am am am
Popeye
spinach eater
lead can ingester
Brutus
the night is bulging
like the black thighs
of hookers
in white pants
he's
a white line
rolling through
his own life
forty-four years
twenty years
here
Los Angeles
his eyes spiral
thru the night
turning down Century Blvd
Manny can feel it too
murder

sweet as raw hamburger
meat
sweet as the pulled
apart pussy lips of a twelve-year-old
his tongue darts out his mouth
like a green snake
everything in him
rises
osmotic
blood
the outside pressure
forcing
the life in
his veins
up out
the sky
the streets
are so wide
rolling rolling
like "Proud Mary"
not like Tina Turner but like
Credence Clearwater
flowing thru
Los Angeles'
black asphalt
his eyes eat the sweat
popping off the nigger's forehead
"You see that Manny!"
"Yeah that coon's up to something!"
The car spins like a top

in the middle
of Century Blvd
only god
can make a U turn here
the sirens rise up
the lights flashing
pump thru the night
red
throbbing
on top the car
salivating bloody light
Get him
                    Git him
transported now
no time
only the chase
like the GTO
in '65
racing
like his heart
in his chest
it feels
so good
wild
something
deep and primitive
is screaming in his toes
the hair under
his arms curls
he slams the door

everywhere is a
movie of light
ALL RITE BUDDY
OUT THE CAR HANDS UP
NO LIP
I'LL BUST YOUR MOTHERFUCKING CHOPS NIGGER
Officer please!
NIGGER
glee rises up
like animal
the night is a circle of sirens
wild tribal
his stick dances
he brings it
down
big black leather
flesh against
flesh he's never
felt so . . . so . . . a yodel
fucks its way
out his mouth
his own smell
covers him
he does his Okie dance
under the pink lights
of Century Blvd
He screams with a joy
you can't steal
or buy

his head is thrown
back
he's connected,
whole—
one
the turning red lights
hit him in the face
and he remembers
fleetingly
the Mexican girl at Steven's.
The nigger's on his knees
Manny is radioing for backup
and the call goes out thru
the star starved night:
      GORILLA
      GORILLA
    GORILLA IN THE MIST.

Gorilla in the Midst #10

Gorilla Gorilla
  Gorilla dick
did you see that nigger's dick?
      Johnson down to his *knees,*
his knees, his dick was down
        to his knees!
Manny wheeled around the corner
    dropped Johnny off
at the bar, brought the vehicle
      back to the station.
Home, he was going home. It
      seemed to sing a song
in him, home. Those stairs, thirteen steps,
      what a number, steps up up
      to someplace else
      alive! Beyond the fucking TV set, beer (although that
helped), the stupid kids
      (how did he ever have motherfuckers so stupid!)
He closed the door on the lie, the truth.
He was just glad the stupid motherfuckers had turned out white! What
would he have done if they hadn't? Bash 'em, bash their little brains
out like the white bitches did during slavery times and what would
Robin's Klan ass have done if she'd found out he wasn't part Greek
and Italian. No, he couldn't have bashed their brains out in the hos-
pital. He woulda had to disappear.

  Like he was gonna
    disappear right now.
      in the familiar blue light of a color glossy life
between the pages of BLACK STUD.

He sucked his teeth
unbuckled his belt
pulled his dick out, decided not to unload his revolver
    sometimes he did, sometimes he didn't
(it was better when he didn't).
    He pulled his pants down,
his dick was getting hard
    he opened the can of motor oil
        its black crazy smell pulling him under car hoods,
down alleys grass stained with motor oil and discarded car parts,
graveyards full of tires and big black men who were mean and warm
and kind. He rubbed the motor oil on his asshole slid the barrel of
the gun up his ass, hoped the gasp that escaped his lips was not audi-
ble. The tension made him bite his lips, the taste of his own blood
excited him like going down on stupid ass when she was on her
period, he liked that. He contracted his sphincter muscles. The barrel
of the gun was still cold, felt good up his ass. He stroked his dick not
ready to start jacking off yet. He felt so good just like he was. From
where he was lying he could see the stack of magazines under the
couch.

He pulled out a glossy magazine, for a second he wondered what
he would do if someone kicked the door in on him or could see him
now, like his partner on the job Johnny or if the stupid motherfucking
kids ever hooked up a video camera and could see him lying here with
his revolver up his ass, his hands, one on his dick, the other holding a
magazine open to its centerfold full of a gargantuan black man as ugly
and beautiful as Mike Tyson, like Charles from the car graveyards
when he was a child.

His right hand became feverish as the beady evil black eyes stared
back at him from the magazine. Past worlds ran through him as the

smell of motor oil poured through his brain. He gasped and semen
shot out on the black face of the centerfold creature. He smiled and
whispered the same thing Johnny had shouted an hour or so ago:

Gorilla, Gorilla

Gorilla in the mist!

Gorilla in the Midst #11

My eye is big
   a giant veined tumor
a viscous snotty
    blob.
It sees
   it watches horror
swing by like a pendulum
    decade after decade
helplessness screaming
    in the wind.
But I only scream
   when it's me, when I'm
the strange fruit.
And tonight I'm not.
   It's not like the nights—
    or is it like the nights
we sat around the fire
drinking my baby's blood.

Drinking my baby's blood?
Shock value?
Nothing shocks us anymore—me, you.
We can talk about this now can't we?
The heart of darkness, the cult, the white people dressed in black, out
under the hills and rolling moon. Can we talk? Can I tell you that my
daddy was a small town chief of police who painted himself blue and
put on a silver star every morning, and a black cape, crucifix, and
saber every night? Can I tell you that we fucked?
    we fucked
    at four five six sixteen,

that we sat around a bonfire
like a Stephen King novel
and called down Satan,
Prince of Darkness,
to sit with us
and slit my baby's throat
mine his
our—
his son, grandson
my son, half brother
all in one
crystal goblet
newborn held up
to the full moon
strange taste
still on my lips
the Addams family on skag
the Munsters on crank.
It's not real,
never happened.
Except once:
I am making the rounds
of every boy in town
during my senior year.
One boy is slower than the rest
to stick it in,
traces the ice scars
on my belly
the almost invisible
tattoos of birth.

He asks me, no tells me,
You had a baby.
Me?
Yeah, you have stretch marks
like my sister from being pregnant.
NO!
No?
I was really fat when I was a kid.
My parents put me on a liquid diet
when I was around twelve.
I lost the weight real fast.
In the end he shut up to get in.
I keep the lights low now.
Don't remember a thing.
Everything normal. Boring.
I forget it all
but tonight it comes back
in this circle of white men in blue
beating this watermelon head nigger
to his knees till he barks
and I remember
the distant glaciers
in my father's eyes
the morning after
buckling his holster
silent over fried eggs, sausage & coffee.
My mother salt.
He slides through the vestibule
pausing at the front door
to lock me in place

with the words that come back
to me tonight
as I watch the LAPD,
the boy's club,
that now includes me.
On his way out the door
to disappear in
his blue duty,
he tells me, Watch your step
or you'll be next.
Crystal goblet
red moon
my silence didn't set me free
but at least I'm alive
not on my knees.
No DNA or video cameras
in those days
all I have is lines like
ice down my stomach
and an eye that now
sees no evil.

August 9th

Hate, black teeth, half an
eyeball, torn light, green grass, dirt
wings. Sick, blind angel.

My Father's Silence (or, Last Night I Hear Two Poets—One Korean, One African American)

The Korean woman reads first
& I hear the torn foot
of war
the bloody footsteps
that connect us
like jewelry around our necks
choking out words, creaking
like my father silent
in his easy chair.
But the photograph talks:
"Korea 1950" written on the back;
black and white, serrated edges
like butterflies. He is tall,
thoughtful, in the blood bleached
green fatigues of war.
A huge tent, the flaps rolled up—
a white man back to the camera
pounds on the typewriter.
Another looks to my father
in deference—up,
like he never has before
in Alabama, Peoria, Mississippi,
San Jose—
like he never will again.
The tent, the jungle foliage—
which are flowers, shrubs & trees
to the natives—
grow forever in a chair, vinyl—
new kinds of plastic crying sounds
we never hear from a silent father

who prides himself on
never talking about the war, *wars,*
there were two.
But I hear in the middle of life
in the barb wire poem of a sun
filled porch they used to drink
iced tea upon & look out on their land—
I hear my father talking
& it is the slow sound
of a man who wants to die.

The black woman reads next—
meat, the kitchen, the Saran Wrap
melting dream of garbage floes
like we couldn't know then, in 1950,
what the aggression would cost us.
The true price of napalm
rolling through the aisle of America
on the wings of a war
that didn't make sense,
he said.
No, he said, silent reactionary
man twisting like a big car
on the huge Erector Sets that haul
automobiles to market,
for a moment, a bump in the road,
& the vehicle, in its trek
from assembly line to grave,
rolls off one time unexpectedly
gumming the works

& a lifetime of petticoats,
Goodyear rubber, file cabinets turn channels
& he says, No,
my sons won't go. And they don't.

He sits silent armchair
of a newspaper dreaming blood barb wire,
the torn integument of the soul
mute in Alabama, Peoria, patient in Mississippi,
passing for white in San Jose
speaks like shrapnel
in the retina of a child's eye,
the fence he couldn't climb
he walks around
twenty years later. The dead
years stacked up like Melmac plates
wrapped in plastic & Styrofoam
even though they can't,
like him, break.
& the gesture is paralyzed
on the fence,
he is blind before he can see
the other side.
In order to die peacefully
he would have had to talk
about things other than
a photograph to his sons.
He would have had to ask
forgiveness,
demand retribution for

the stolen snapshot of his soul.
Somewhere the wings of a butterfly
needed to be rearranged;
as it was
he walked along the fence
the major fold in his brain
dividing the days & the nights
choking on Saran Wrap with
petticoats dark as nuclear winter
frozen on the little legs
of a tricycle.

Benin Silver Father Slaves

In the ancient kingdom of Benin water was the realm
of the ancestors; it was seen as a mirror reflection
of the land of the living. So where is my father?
Is he waiting for me under the water.
Will he approve of me or beat me or love me,
or even know me. In the kingdom of Benin metal

was traded for pepper, ivory, and finally slaves. Metal—
brass, silver. History lives in the realm
of the imagination as much as dreams. How does "me"
arrive in this equation? How does the reflection
of my culture shine on me? Slaves across the water,
the trauma of racism. My father

did not particularly like the word black. My father
would grow up to acquire metal,
then what escape and peace it could buy. If water
brought us here, and it did, *and,* it is the realm
of the ancestors—where's my mother? The reflection
in the mirror this morning is somewhere beyond me.

The construction of the African American me
goes back over the water, past father,
Daddy. So much of my life has been a reflection
of that decision to trade flesh for metal.
My life has been lived in the realm
of shame, I look to water, water

to heal, water to cleanse. Water
to nourish. Though I think honesty is what will heal me—

honesty and the courage to feel again. The realm
of the ancestors, if it's water and my father
is there, he is there without the metal—
wedding ring or gun. He is bathing in the reflection

of a young boy's dreams. When we look at his reflection
it is of a boy without shoes or shame. Water
can be polluted. The history of Benin was preserved in metal,
stolen by the British, put in museums. Now it is me,
centuries from home taking notes in a museum, learning my father
is in the water, an ancestor, in another realm.

In the morning's mirror the reflection goes into the realm
of the land of the dead. In my lips, my jaw I see my father,
metal, and ships upon water. Did he ever really love me?

Looking at Plate No. 4:
"Homicide Body of John Rodgers, 883 W. 134th Street, Christensen, October 21, 1915"

in *Evidence* by Luc Sante

I'm looking at the
   big black
      hands of death
on the immaculate tile design
   of blood on footprints,
      the shine of shoes in corners
   the stalwart jaw
of a witness.
   I'm looking at a century
      inching into being
         I'm looking at a photograph
of a black man
   sixty-five years after slavery
      lying on a floor dead—
         hat dropped
            like a felt
               bomb
round perfect boulder like it was
   In 1915
      everything
         (nothing)
            had happened yet—
            Give us time
               and every river
                  is the seven of Hiroshima.

I'm looking at the feet
    pointed like poison
        like the prince's sword
to a picture
    poured half full
        last night's red wine
the mother, cutpurse,
    on videotape
        the ancient castle
of a drama
    now a book report
        for school.
        King killed
          by his brother
in Memphis 1968
    poison poured in his ear.
I'm looking at the square
    corners
        of a big man's jaw
gaped open, the pointed
    teeth of death ape-like
        in the buck eyes
of permanent surprise.
    I'm looking at
        the tiles turn to the
          chain fence
            the German shepherd
of a dark afternoon

six million frozen
    forever in
the dark white night
  of the Holocaust
    blowing like the backhand
of god looking
  at a photograph in
    the comfortable overcoat
of an automobile moving
  past the past
    stuck in the rigor mortis
of one black man's body
  in America with
    his penis outside history
     hanging in
the bad light
  of magnolia
    trees bent to the ground
with the sound
    of hat
     after velvet hat
crashing like tattoos
     in time.

A Window Opens

It is like the curtains have been thrown open in front
a large window suffused with light. The memory is very clear—
you are large, shining, naked—all penis
trying for my mouth. I am around four
years old. You are around forty. Dead now,
you have been dead now almost eight years.

Eight years, and then a window opens and the years
disappear like that and I am in front
your naked body, a child. What to say now
to the nice man I am having tea with, clear
he is not a perpetrator but still a man. And I'm not four
and I want it, in my cunt, mouth, his penis.

It's not the devil or my higher power, his penis.
But I seem far away now—years
from a man's love. I wonder what this has all been for—
the women I hid in and could not love, the lesbian front
that became a wall, the sex work. It is clear
I was not cut out for bulldyking or prostitution now.

But now what, what now?
I have lived without so much, I could live without his penis.
I could just go back to what I wasn't, but the picture was so clear,
as though I was standing in front an open window. Years
I have sought sex, avoided love, closeness, presented a front—
the old bulls stop me on the train, street. I am four

looking in a window at my father and a four-
year-old. The old bulls want to rub and lick my cunt now—

all my money, fame, and I won't put them up front
after climbing on their fat backs, I want a penis!
What do I have after all these years
of avoidance? I think of Rumi's poem, the clear-

ing, beyond right doing and wrong doing—clear
field. I'll meet you there, you, who are for
me? It is late, I think hours, minutes, not years!
What do I want now?
To love? It's not really about a penis—
It's about opening, being vulnerable, coming out front

with my desire, being clear after all these years. The front
is as big as the back. I am not four, his penis
is not my father's. My father is dead, it's my life now.

My Father Meets God
(or, The Dream of Forgiveness)

Such a godly thing this forgiveness. It's like that scene in *Cabin in the Sky*. You are at the pearly gates and like, Louis Armstrong or whoever was St Peter, is out the picture. Knobby knees denting your blue and white striped pajamas, ashy feet, no toupee, you are talking to God. She is, as we didn't know she would be, an overweight Samoan woman! She was born in San Francisco, hung out with African American people, talks like she's black, so this, I guess, is how she gets in *Cabin in the Sky?* That is a question, not an explanation. One thing you can see is she has my mouth! Jesus, she is me! Maybe a past life or some shit? Anyway, she is God, and she is talking to you. She is telling you, God is telling you, she loves you. She is thanking you for the burst of white light that was the sperm that began her life. She thanks you. She thanks you for the money Daddy. She says she paid off the school loans. Quit that sun up to sun down job that you ran, barefoot on a dirt road, away from when you were fourteen years old in 1929; third, second? generation out of slavery, running from a crazy man who beat you, with his foot on your neck till your nose bleeds. God says when she got the money she bought some records, pizza with pepperoni, some clothes— like always, like a nigger. A leather coat, arming me against insolvency, bad credit, bounced checks, runaway debt, a mattress on the floor, roaches. But I pay them back Daddy. I stop Haggle and Haggle from garnishing my check, get off the hot coals they're dragging me across, get 'em off my back. Know I sent many a Princess to prep school with that two thousand dollar principal that rose like generations in ignorance to twelve thousand dollars and lawyers fees. Fuck it! I just give 'em back their fucking money. Call it restitution. If I ever harmed you, America, if slavery didn't take enough, take it motherfucker! Daddy, God knew you would want her to go back to school, knew you did not believe we were genetically inferior and could learn and get a good job. She knew you would want her to join a pantyhosed, be-pearled, per-

fumed, middle class despite everything. You believed in denial as a sur-
vival mechanism, that every day was a new day, what was past was past,
they talked about Jesus Christ didn't they, you told me when I told you
people talked about you. I remember when you said Michael could turn
his life around, that plenty of men get out of prison and go on to do
something with their lives. He could make it today if he wanted, you
had said. Look, do you have much of a chance to talk to him now? Well,
maybe after you've been around awhile. So, Daddy, I cut the mustard
you were always talking about (though I never quite understood where
that expression came from). I made my mark, my first one at least.
Make your mark! you would always say. I remembered what you said,
all that stuff—a man could walk out of prison, out of the past, and turn
his life around.

I knew you weren't talking about me, but I remembered what you
said, and *it*. I decided not to let it hold me back. I walked away from it
by walking into it.

Look look Daddy God is showing a movie. It's your life. She's play-
ing it back for you. See there's your mother's thin legs cocked open
your head is breaking her apart for the last time, you the seventh son of
a son of a gun! Aries born to rule! Born to rise. Look Daddy, there you
are, the brightest, the tallest boy the youngest boy. Look at you running,
look how you strive. Look look see Daddy see the flag red white and
blue. See you in a uniform defending it see see the woman her legs open
like your mother giving birth. The nurse says it's a girl! Sergeant
Lofton. You are happy. A girl is great, almost as good as a boy! She
can't play football but she can be a nurse or teacher be a cheerleader, go
to Mills or Spellman. She's not gonna be light but she's not gonna be
too dark or have a big nose. She has no excuse for being fat you will tell
her, neither of her parents are. This is your girl. She is properly dressed
and plays with plastic dolls. She loves them, like you do Polaroid.

Daddy Daddy come quick, it's forty! It's forty, the film starts to go faster, same life but it's slipping by you even as you rise to the top Daddy Daddy God is talking, very gently but she's talking LOOK LOOK she turns your head toward the movie screen, your life. She says only God (and she is God) can change it. She says, What Emanuel Millard, like your mama named you, she says, Billy, like your mama called you, she says, Michael like you named yourself, or Mike like you asked the fellas to call you. She says is there anything you'd like to change this is your last chance. And you tell her STOP STOP go back. There's a night a day nights days, my daughter, daughters, lie about. Make my daughter, especially Ramona, Sapphire—I like that name actually. Her mama named her Ramona, I didn't have no say in it. Change it, you hiss, change it, make my girl stop lying. Change it, or—or can you erase that? God says what would you give to change that? You say, I'd go back, back, all the way back under the ocean beyond the middle passage, I'd go to the land of cut Achilles, amputated clitorises, mules and men with no tongues, I'd go to where all the tongues that have been cut off go, where blind eyes go. I'd go to grass, I'd go to being a one-celled organism. I'd do anything to stop the lying or—or change what I did, if I did anything like that. God? God, I'm talking to you. God looks at him, looks around, it's more like *The Johnny Otis Show* now than *Cabin in the Sky*. Esther Phillips is up there singing:

> *I'm going to Chicago*
> *and I'm sorry I can't take you*

God, I always sat at the table with the white people. I never could understand why the colored boys in the service always sat together. Me, I would go get my tray and sit at the table with the white soldiers. You know, I'm surprised I'm so happy you're colored! What are you? Colored. Well, whatever, you look black sort of. I'm happy. Is it because you want forgiveness? she asks. No, it's because you're so pretty. God, his voice is pleading now, Can you change it? Yes, she says, it is changed. Are you sure? Yes, says God. I know you're God but give me some proof! Oh Lord! You men! she says, then snaps, What year is it? Year? Yes, what year is it? Why, it's the day I died, it's November 20, 1990. OK, you want proof? Yes God, you—I believed in you and Jesus. I still believe in you even though you uhh look, are, so different. So, what did you want proof of exactly. That—that night—those days— that—that something has changed? You know that even though I'm God I can't change the past. Wha . . . wha . . . , he sputters, you lying wench! Why did you say you could if you couldn't! Well, because be- ing God I could and did. Double talk! could what? did what? Either you can or you can't. Either you did or you didn't. First it's, Yeah yeah any- thing you want. Now it's this funny stuff, "Even though I'm God I can't change the past." So why did you say you could if you couldn't? Well, because being God I did. Did what? Change it, I changed it for you. How? The way you change the past. Look Daddy, I'm gonna roll the film forward Daddy. Look look Daddy see your girl run. Look look Daddy see your girl deposit that big check. Look at your girl lift up the people; she's the nurse, teacher (poet/healer) you always wanted her to be. Look look see Sapphire shine. She changed it for you, the past. That's what children are for. Look look she's walking—Where? It looks like, yeah, that's Fourteenth Street in New York. She's singing. She can't sing! Why not? Well, I can't sing, it runs in the family. Well, what could she do? I wanted to be a poet you know. Yes, I know. What's she singing and how come I can't hear her if you can hear her. Don't be silly, I'm God and her, of course I can hear her. You're just ah, ah, you know, dead guy. I didn't mean that the way it sounded, she said. Any- way, she's singing that Billie Holiday song— You know I saw Billie

Holiday at the Apollo. Count Basie, Ella—where's my daughter going, what's she singing?

> *Mama may have*
> *Papa may have*
> *But God bless the child that's got his own*

And where's she going? She's on her way to the bank— My bank? Where I used to work? You know I was personnel manager for twenty years— I know. I got a pension from the army and the bank and I own my house. Is that the one you put her out of— I'm sorry. That's the one they'll sell, and she'll pay off her student loans and go back to school on. I'm glad. I know you are. Where you say she's going God? She going to work? No, right now she's going to the bank to cash in. She works for me now you know. You? She ain't dead! No, I ain't dead. I'm God. You're dead Daddy and your girl she works for me, God. What she do? She talks with the cut out tongue you gave her, she comes with the amputated clitorises, she runs on the severed Achilles, she flies man. She's a poet. What's she doing? I can't see so clear. She's still singing. What? A new song, something different— Different from the past? Yes, I told you the past is changed— But then you said you can't change the past— She changed it. Look, see see, how the past changes, advances into the future— You know I went blind before I died— I know but you ain't blind no more! Shucks, may as well be, I'm dead! You're dead but now you can see. You can see what you did and what you didn't do. She's alright. Your girl is alright. You hurt her, hurt her bad, but you didn't kill her. Slowed her down some, but you didn't stop her. Thank God! Oh, thank God! You're welcome.

Indians

In the dream there are three people, bows and arrows
one person bent over the two—a feeling of combat;
there are also people dressed in the color white.
The cat crawls next to me rubbing his back
against this book. That is not part of the dream.
Everything must change nothing stays the same.

Your body, life—nothing stays the same.
Who would have the bows and arrows?
Waking up stops the action of a dream;
the land is always locked in mortal combat.
And when we have won, they've taken it back.
It is true there is no such thing as being white—

They made it up, a social construction, white
saved them, starving people, thieves, debtors; the same
people who were niggers in their lands climbed on the back
of people colored differently. The Indians, bows and arrows,
less than ½ of 1 percent of today's population. The combat
is now in books, memories, the flurry of dreams.

Lately I have not entered the land of my dreams.
In this place the color white
was something people were dressed in. The combat
now is in my soul—to grow and not to be ambushed by the same
ideas that stopped my parents—the arrows
of indecision, guilt, and the monkey on their back.

Her alcoholism, the dark memories embedded in his back.
There is a difference between dreams

and fantasy. Fantasy is fat and honey on your tongue. But the
    arrow
into subconscious, the hidden or blinded desire could be dressed
    in white
in a dream. Some things remain the same—
like the need to grow and change. My father saw combat.

I am engaged now with myself in combat.
I am fighting to win my self-respect and -love back—
I was born with them. I don't want to remain the same.
There is no girl who is me in my dream—
let that change. Let the people dressed in white
be healers. Let me be penetrated and not killed by his arrow.

Native people once 100 percent of the population—combat, bows
    and arrows—
become named "Indians" in America's justified genocide—white.
But they keep coming back like the Palestinians, niggers—the
    vanquished dream.

#1 of Many: In the Dream

In the dream it's black
   like a snake
big
    winding around
      somebody's torso
         in the dream
     I'm not seen
       in the light
     by the young boy
       as old
     in the dream
        I have my life
       like footsteps laid
         out before me
           in the dream
       I run on
          place my feet
            in the footsteps
to fly away to blue
      but wake up sitting at my desk
          in Texas. The subject is, as usual, Little Black Sambo
& from the bottom of the swimming pool where she will drown drunk
in 1962 the teacher is telling me I'm a fool because I would vote
for Kennedy because I think he is cute.
        Outside the window, the grass
           is green
       Ft Hood, Texas
        1961

             . . .

ballet class
    a girl like a princess,
Sandy W., perfect
    blond bun on her head, her legs
opening like pink dreams
    below her black leotard—
to ballet, her promised hand on
    the bar. She is nine years old too,
      Prima princess, the pea under the mattress is
        you will be forty-four years old one day too,
bleed every month and watch
    crow's feet land on your face,
      men go or stay too long
You will flatten or fatten
    out under a southern sky
even if you run
  my pen has you here at nine
    in a leotard the yolk
      of my black envy
spread out under a blue blue sky
  black like the snake
    or the Haitian boy's uncircumcised
penis hiding in the pink pink sky of a tourist's painting
    behind the fence I look over at my father
walking down the street with me
  as if he is noble &
    loves me no matter what, the way
a crater is in my life
  the way even joy is lived in the dark

    penumbra of knowing
the possible miotic division
     of evil
rising between my eyes with no name
except hole blue tongue slit at the tip of a penis
crossed like a dirt road rocking like a guitar in the shape
of a car fourteen years old cracked across the incisors of a de-
                    cayed center
of blue fields

Some Different Kinda Books

I

She asks why we always
read books about black people.
(I spare her the news she is black.)
She wants something different.
Her own book is written in pencil.
She painstakingly goes back & corrects
the misspelled words.
We write each day.
Each day the words look like
a retarded hand from Mars
wrote them.
Each day she asks me how
do you spell: didn't, tomorrow, done
husband, son, learning, went, gone . . .
I can't think of all the words she can't spell.
It's easier to think of what she can spell:
MY NAME IS CARMEN LOPEZ.
I am sorry I was out teacher.
My husband was sick.
You know I never miss school.
In that other program
I wasn't learning nothing.
Here, I'm learning so I come.
What's wrong with my husband?
I don't know. He's in the hospital. He's real sick
I was almost out the room
when I hear the nurse ask him,

Do you do drugs?
He say yes.
I say what!
I don't know nuthin' 'bout no drugs.
I'm going off in the hospital.
He's sick.
I'm mad.
Nobody tells you nuthin'!
I didn't hear that nurse
I wouldn't know
nuthin'.
Huh?
Condoms? No, teacher.
He's my husband.
I never been with another man.

II

I think he got AIDS
he still don't tell me.
I did teacher. I tried
to read the chart at the hospital
but I couldn't figure out those words.
Doctor don't say, he say privacy.
The nurse tell me.
She's Puerto Rican. She say your husband
got AIDS.
I go off in the hospital.
Nobody tells me nuthin'.

He come home.
He say it's not true,
he's fine.
He's so skinny without his clothes
he try to hide hisself nekkid
don't want me to look.
I say you got to use
one of those things.
He say nuthin's wrong.
with him.

III

He stop sayin' that.
Now he just say he's gonna die
all the time
all the time
dying.
I say STOP that talk,
the doctor say you could
live a long time
my sister-in-law say,
he got it so you got it
it's like that.
I say, I don't got it,
my kids don't got it either.
Teacher, I need a letter for welfare
that I'm coming to school
on a regular basis.

IV

He's in P.R.,
before that he started messing around
again.
Over the Christmas holidays
he died.
That's where I was at
in P.R.
I'm fine. Yeah, I'm sure teacher.
What do *I* wanna do teacher?
I just wanna read some different
kinda books.

Found Poem
(in the *New York Times* in an article written by
James C. McKinley Jr. on Rwanda)

"The dead," the doctor says, "are speaking to us."

some skeletons will be enclosed in a glass case
inside the church as a permanent reminder

the doctors move quietly through the church in nylon
surgical suits and masks. They have set up an X-ray
table powered by a generator in a corner of the church.
and behind the building in a tent, a modern autopsy room
     with three operating tables.
inside the chapel the bodies are laid out between pews
     each in a numbered bag.

the killers worked at close range with machetes and clubs.
"You had to be looking the person in the eye, basically,
     to do it."

the bones tell a violent history of their last moments

a few had their Achilles tendons cut

#467, a young man, about 20 years old
his left hand is cut across the knuckles
another machete blow
drove deep into his hip
through the ball and socket
and cut a good four inches into his pelvic bone
crippling him

his shoulder shoulder shoulder blades
have similar similar similar cuts
where his attackers came down
on his back
splitting it open to the bone.
Finally, there is the mortal wound—
a gash on the left side of his skull
that crushed the eye socket socket socket and
drove into his brain.

Chava, Catalogue Chairs, & Three Colored Scarves

Hanging on the back of three kitchen chairs
are three kerchiefs—yellow, red, magenta squares
that I fold neatly into little rectangles when I arise.
I am trying to restore order
after forty-five seconds of chaos, screaming
in the night. It happens like a grocery bag splitting

in the rain everything falling. The present actions splitting
you from your future. I remember when I bought the chairs,
mail order, a thousand dollars or some shit. Toosie screaming
is Chava, is a thousand women screaming. Who are the squares
when everyone has a story? Last night I arise
scream on a neighbor's doorstep, You stupid niggers! in order

to try and restore, to the night they are killing, order
quiet, the stealthy silence, they are splitting
with construction work. This morning I arise
to the memory of screaming. On the back of kitchen chairs
I hung fresh washed kerchiefs to dry, squares
of colored cotton, order in the midst of women screaming.

In the hospital she realizes it saved her life, screaming
when the madman came breaking the morning's order
with his knife. I fold rectangles from squares,
Antwerp crosses my mind, anything but the air splitting
with a young dancer's stab wounds. The chairs
are uncomfortable I couldn't see that in the catalogue. Aris-

ing, there is only a tiny speck of black. I remember when I arise
what I have done. Last night in an orange shirt and panties screaming

Stop the motherfucking noise. At home the table and chairs
charged and delivered to me useless. He intended to kill her. In order
to make sense of her life, almost healing, then her stomach splitting
opens again, the scar tissue, the rectangle back to a square,

she has had to keep moving, had to find triangles in squares,
build pyramids. I find the empty bottle when I arise,
99 cent bottle of nail polish. I see myself splitting,
in a little while I will read my own writing, a woman screaming
under a razor blade coming down like a windmill turning the order
of morning into an issue of blood. I don't like the chairs.

Red, yellow, and magenta squares hanging on the back of kitchen
    chairs
I remember how order breaks in a second, splitting, I arise
think to dispose of the bottle, remember Chava screaming.

Waldsterben

Waldsterben, in German, it is the dying of the woods
I dream of rice plants, a circle, things growing.
Awake from the dream I see a man
riding a bicycle across a snowy tundra
I am drenched, no, just damp, with sweat.
Yesterday I do a reading, answer questions from journalists.

I am now used to talking to journalists
if you dream of dying in the woods
is that a lack of love? For a long time I did not sweat.
But now I wake up sweating, dreaming rice plants growing.
I have talked before about the wolf, the tundra
salt, the knife. The wolf and man.

The trap set for the wolf by man.
I am kind, thoughtful, considerate with journalists.
It is snowing, or snow is blowing on the tundra,
or at least that is what I think and there are no woods.
There is a circle beyond which there is no growing,
except moss; it's just too cold. I imagine your sweat

could freeze and kill you. As I said, I did not sweat
much as a kid, or even when I was older with a man.
In New York they are dying and growing,
the trees. What can I compare the journalists
to? Hunters in the woods?
A wolf on the tundra?

A dog sled is one thing but a bicycle across the tundra.
A bicycle, a man with an Adidas sweat

suit. Then a trapper, and a wolf in the woods.
Salt, the wolf wants salt. The man
wants the wolf or his skin. The journalist
too wants you or your skin. I think of Oscar's story growing

underneath his grandmother's skirt. I think of potatoes growing
then the line where the growing stops, the tundra
snow blowing, a dog sled pulling some silly journalists
who freeze or get shot, their sweat
souring in death. I think of the razor the man
places inside the slab of salt, the wolf in the woods.

I think of New York, trees growing, a tongue in the woods
slashed red blanket on the tundra. And I see a man
on a bicycle, pedaling from journalists, drenched in sweat.

Black Wings

Moon, breasts, dark sores
open black wings expectation
sidereal light twice

Dark Sores

Dark sores black wings of expectation
what is sidereal light twice?
I meet hope at the train station

Whistle blows, tracks rattle, I run
down someplace forty years, a wedding, rice.
Dark sores black wings of expectations.

You are connected like a generation
in white blouses trying to be nice.
Hope is at the train station.

Fat palm trees, tan briefcase, vacation
a million miles from every night
dark sores. Black wings of expectation.

We're girls, just wanna have fun!
The wedding rice turns to beans every night
you slip out seek hope at the station

tell him you're alone, on vacation
that there is a sidereal light.
Dark sores black wings of expectation
open and meet hope at the train station.

Leave the Lights On

It is an act of courage to say, Leave the lights on.
There is actually everything to hide
Flaccid, distended, forty-seven, so much is gone.

If I had gone to the gym, had the tumors operated on
perhaps I could have displayed my body with more pride.
As it is, it is an act of courage to leave the lights on.

And, truthfully, I'm curious to see, now that beauty is gone,
what will be reflected in a man's eyes.
Flaccid, belly distended with tumors, so much is gone.

But still the ugly body is love's sweet swan.
Love doesn't ask one to be blind or hide.
It is an act of courage to leave the lights on.

Oh! He doesn't even have a condom!
It is in my hard muscular courage I take pride.
Breasts flaccid, gut distended, at forty-seven so much is gone.

But inside the fat egg is the black swan.
My throat opens like wings between your thighs.
It is an act of courage to say, Leave the lights on.
Nothing essential, but still, so much *is* gone.

bleeding from the head

the black ears of a cat
rising over the light
left in the dark throat
of memorized money
she fell into the GAP
to earn working class values
and a footprint,
a drop of blood
on a boy's Levi's,
ties her to death
with a screwdriver
twisted past function
in her white throat
of everybody's
so shopped at the
grey GAP on the floor wrists
taped to the life
you would have led
if you hadn't been the
peaches and cream
of a bowl of grits stolen
in the mind of an
IRT emergency cord
rocking around the clock
of a lie that eats
the dream of tulle blue
courtroom dust off
the Kansas red shoes
dipped in the silver paint
of an HIV status marching

down the artery of a third
rail placating the dying
blond wish of a tarot
deck stuffed up the stink
of light rolled over on its
belly—Our father you oughtta
shit in here
decorate the venereal warts
of time sliced across
the cornea of a corner
in Watts tarred over like
the gunfinger pushed
back to Neptune's porno
penny of rolled joint loose
on the edge of vial in class-
rooms where we suck
the dick of light cracked
in the lavatory of cold
tile washing the sound of
death around our ears
like burglar alarms singing
the low level of video education
bent twice over the toilet
of fission flushing the sweet
shit of a dream piling up
like used light recycled in
the green nipple ring
of chloroform pellets dropping
to the sound of a bleach
so sweet it can turn

the bones of darkness into
jungle gyms of wet dog
tongues lapping up the
sold urine on a gymnasium
of plastic turf divided into
kill 'em now or kill 'em later
downtown let's fuck around
twisting the night away
'90s style screwdrivers
of eyes seeing the back-
wards bend of progress
broken like the rusted
nail of Jesus' penis
driven through the dog eye
of light dropping
like a savage beast
in Bethlehem.

"Who are those other two people?" she asked

"Who are those other two people?" she asked
about the figures in the picture. Your children,
I have to explain to my mother. The pictures
in movies get mixed up with pictures in dreams.
"Open your mouth!" He is made to open his mouth
on the curb, lying prostrate in the street

open black mouth seeming about to bite the street
curb. Gun to his head. You wouldn't have asked
what next? Because you thought you knew. Then his open mouth
is crushed into the curb. I don't say, Your children,
bitch; I say Angie and Michael. This was one of my dreams,
to be able to wake up in the morning, write. But not of pictures,

of a boot coming down on a black man's face. The picture
they showed my father wasn't like in the movies. They scraped him
     off the street,
took a Polaroid. No morgue like in the movies. One of my dreams
as a child was to be a movie star. Is that your son, they asked.
Marilyn Monroe, Butterfly McQueen, the 1950s; what do children
know? I didn't know I was black, that his mouth

would be a home for fly eggs, that his mouth
would teem with maggots. Get the picture?
"She didn't fight for you children,
for *you*," the therapist says. Sometimes in the street

I see a mouse-like woman that could be her. She asked
me for money when I went to see her. In my dreams

I'm safe. I don't see my mother in my dreams.
In the mirror it's my father's curvaceous mouth
I put the lipstick on. I don't think she ever asked
about my brother. Last night the picture—
the man's open mouth, lying on the street
a second before death, reminds me somehow of being children,

the boot behind our neck inconceivable because we are children.
Our frame of reference, our dreams, even in our dreams
we cannot comprehend that much evil—that you'll die in the
    street,
My Lai, Jonestown, Jimi's vomit unable to make it out his mouth.
When I looked through her things, the pictures
were mostly of herself. I couldn't find the one I'd asked

her for. Drunk. Street. Dreams. Well, where'd you stay, I'd
    asked
her once. Here and there, she'd said. She'd kept the pictures
taken, "Before you children were born!" The lipstick not yet a blur
    on her mouth.

saw James Brown

saw James Brown
yesterday
I stop
for crowd
gathered around
the Apollo
who? who?
James Brown!
first it's his wife
the one the *National Enquirer*
says he beat
with a lead pipe.
The wife
is lighter
than she appears
in photographs
a flash
of red suit
lips
a wall
of makeup
big hair
bust
built up like Dolly Parton.
Creole-looking woman
five feet tall.
Then him
dark shining
made up
compact ·

the paunch
sitting behind
a leather belt
& black turtleneck
the GODFATHER
in patent leather curls
& silver-grey
sharkskin
his smile an ivory beacon
flashing
in the darkness
of his face
the people
reach
out their
hands
for the legend
his hand is slow
he moves
thru
the past to the
new limousine
ancient
already
his obituary
known:
a long list of black men
appearing in
America
rise fall rise

recover fall
get out of jail
the people
the hands
held out
always
there
125th Street
we gather
round
drowning
out the clang
of a jail cell
door shutting
bad press
the woman screaming
he hit me
drugs
you're the same
as us but different
phoenix
not consumed
by the fire
we are
burning
burning
in.

Neverland

I remember Michael Jackson—
perfect shiny shy round brown button
of a boy, who just wanted to dance,
& dance he did, like light spinning
in shoes—

        turning turning

                till his reflection
arrests him & he stops.

Michael stops in front the mirror
and says:

        I will
        I have the will
        to change
            My face
I want my face different.
He looks at his nostrils flaring
fire like horses & his lips & his chin
& his eyes & his cheekbones
& he says I want, I want
a nose that glows white, that glows thin
& long & white.
I want it & I shall
have it!
Everybody wants it, so shut up!
It's just everybody can't have it is all
But I can have it.

I can have it.

Why does he hit me
& I'm a millionaire?
Why does he hit me & my feet
are the golden eggs that bought
the farm, the ranch, the mansions,
the zoo?
Why does he hit me?
I'm so very smart
I buy those old songs of John & Paul
& Ringo & sell 'em for dog food
commercials. I am rich.
I don't want to be hit
Do you hear me Father?
Father
I pray
I am devout
vegetarian
Jehovah's Witness
I dance till I collapse
in a pool of lost sex & sweat
I light the world
Platinum boy
channel
singing "Billy Jean"
"Thriller"

I sell sell *sell*
my success is phenomenal.
I have a friend. A lovely
friend. He is a Witness too.
He doesn't eat meat either.
We are special as fresh carrot juice
& the maids who turn
back our sheets.
He is a lightning boy
& when I'm with him I'm not the scarecrow
or a billion dollar brown wind-up doll
I put my tongue on him
taste the life in his nipples
penis
he is splendiferous.

Father, NO!
I'm a millionaire
I have houses
Get that faggot out of here!
His fist rearranges my sight
& for a while all I see
is his voice writing
like the blimp he is
across the sky:
There'll be no freakish shit
in this house
What are you!

What are you!
Some kinda fairy-ass
faggot!

No, Father
no father.

I wrap myself in a sparkling white glove.
A hand I reach out that touches no one,
separated now like I am from the soft
velvet of his balls,
hard round of his chest—
memories erased like chalkboards
in elementary school
like the questions in the early years to Barry
about where all the money went.
I'm vacant now, a channel.

Still it fills me sometimes
like wanting something more than
monkeys & a ranch
& I just dance harder
till I pass out
& I pass out every time
the semen
spirit rises up
like a shaman & takes my soul
under the lights

& I'm not human. I'm a phenomenon
a miracle of motion going back to Indiana
Los Angeles Motown light sound
breaking into a tornado
of rhythm
wanting wanting
what I can't have.

Fairy Tale #1
(or, Little Red Riding Hood Revisited)

incest is the wolf.
denial is the forest
your mother sends you through.
the red cape is the passion,
the cloak of the warrior.
the brave woodcutter (and this is the catch)
the brave woodsman,
who slays the wolf,
and saves you,
will have to be yourself.

the life you lead will be the one
you carve out.
will the red cloak fit,
will you like the food in the basket?
maybe you will take the wolf's tongue
into your mouth and go willingly to a
house made of gingerbread.
why did your mother send you
in the first place to do the job
that was hers?
will you chop off your own
toes with the ax?
will you get hung up on the
weird berries growing like
little red nipples
on the underside of shiny green leaves?

the ax
the path

the cape
the shoes
the mother
the forest
the wolf
the woodcutter
the grandmother—
you were given these.
how will you rearrange, tell back the story
through time?
what choices do you really have
when the story's so old?
is the moss soft under your feet?
is there mystery in that much green?
do you take the woodcutter in?
and *who, who,* hoots the owl
holds a girl child whose eyes have been
plucked out and sent into the forest alone?

I keep going

but I don't want to write about
how the air stinks with the smell
of loneliness.
how it beats me like some Tonton Maconte hand
from Haiti
how it shoots me in the back like some
Israeli settler bent on the final
solution
how it has no flag or homeland.
how it walks outside the night
dragging a penis of ice,
eyes like empty cans.
it got my brother
it got my mother
it got my father
it has my sister's foot in its mouth
I see the top of a hill, the blue sky over it
either way—his hill, my hill, I keep going.

Today

Today is the day you have been waiting for
when you would finally begin to live
when you would at last open the door

This is the *what,* the circumstance, the *more*
you have been withholding, saving to give.
Today is the day you have been waiting for

when you could sit down to your desk for
hours, take pride, time, find out what work is,
when you would at last open the door

to your own self-development, what god has for
you. Today is the day you come out of prison, live.
Today is the day you've been waiting for

the tomorrow you pined away yesterday for.
I think love rhymes in a way with give.
You at last open the door

to the possibility of now, the core
of life is the moment, now, how you live.
Today is the day I have been waiting for
when you would at last open the door

Broken

I think everything in me has been broken. The shiny ceramic red heart lies on the floor in shards, its light that used to flash electric now glows steady in the dark. Outside the window I watch the souls of my mother and father wrapped in black shawls ride down the river, weird water, in strange boats. They are without hearts, liver, feet—except soles, they are all souls now. I am here in my time, lit, broken, fire burning, full of holes. Vibrating, at last, light, life, mine. At last, broken.

Notes

PAGES 3–19 *"Breaking Karma #5" through "#9":* "Breaking Karma #1" through "#4" appeared in *American Dreams* (Vintage, 1994), my first book of poetry.

PAGES 57–72 *"Gorilla in the Midst #7" through "#11":* "Gorilla in the Midst #1" through "#6" appeared in *American Dreams* (Vintage, 1994).

The "Gorilla in the Midst" poems, satiric poetic vignettes exploring sexual stereotypes, issues of power, and racism, began as a meditation on the public rumor that in the 1960s some members of the Los Angeles Police Department began their tour of duty singing, "Let's shoot a nigger tonight"—a bastardization of Lucky Strike's cigarette jingle "Let's smoke a Lucky tonight!"—and then devoted the tour of duty to the random pursuit and murder of a black man instead of to crime fighting. And of course it was documented and revealed to the public in the early 1990s that members of the LAPD, upon sighting a black male, would call out over the radio to other patrol cars, "Gorilla in the Mist! Gorilla in the Mist!"

PAGES 78–79 *"Benin Silver Father Slaves":* This poem owes much to a series of lectures on African art given by Alisa LaGamma at the Metropolitan Museum of Art, New York, in 1998.

PAGES 80–82 *"Looking at Plate No. 4: 'Homicide Body of John Rodgers, 883 W. 134th Street, Christensen, October 21, 1915,'" in* Evidence *by Luc Sante:* This particular poem is a meditation on two photographs in Luc Sante's compilation of photographs taken by the New York City Police Department between 1914 and 1918. In this collection—mostly of homicide victims—two pictures in particular commanded my attention: plate 4, for which the poem is titled, and by which I found out that the homicide had occurred, some eighty years ago, across the street from where I sat writing in my apartment on Lenox Avenue in Harlem; and plate 14, a picture of another African American male homicide victim, who, unlike any of the other victims, was photographed with his penis deliberately exposed.

"Once again, the undressing is undoubtedly the work of police or doctors, but if the victim had been white the responsible parties would unquestionably have tucked his penis back into his pants" (Luc Sante, *Evidence,* page 71).

PAGES 83–84 *"A Window Opens":* The lines quoted in the poem are from the Persian poet Rumi [1207–73]:

> Out beyond ideas of wrong doing and right doing,
> there is a field. I'll meet you there.

Despite being internationally known as a lesbian ("lesbian icon," according to one publication), I no longer live as, or call myself, a lesbian (or a homosexual). Which brings up the much-debated topic, in the homosexual community, of biological determinism, the theory that people are genetically predetermined to engage in same-sex or opposite-sex acts or relationships, and that as with eye color or skin color, they have no choice and are not able to change.

For me lesbian separatism was an identity chosen because of a desire to be free of men and male oppression (they were one and the same to me). But what began as a separatist and man-loathing identity, based on avoidance and escapism, evolved into a journey on which I began to heal myself from the trauma of childhood sexual abuse. Part of that healing has been being able to, after the devastation and betrayal of rape and childhood sexual abuse, love men again.

PAGES 90–91 *"Indians":* I am indebted to Joy Harjo, *Furious Light,* Watershed Tapes, C-192, for the devastating quote "Native Americans were one hundred percent of the population a few years ago. Today they are one half of one percent of the population." "Indians" also owes much to the ideas promulgated by John Garvey and Noel Ignatiev in their ferocious and uncompromising journal *Race Traitor: a journal of new abolitionism.* There is also a debt and a promise not to forget to the young Palestinian American author of *Born Palestinian, Born Black,* Suheir Hammad.

PAGES 99–100 *"Found Poem":* A found poem is one in which the poet "finds" the text to his or her poem within another text. Most found poems are taken, as is this one, almost verbatim from the found text—in this case, a *New York Times* article written by James C. McKinley Jr. about the genocidal slaughter of 800,000 to 1 million Rwandan Tutsis in the Republic of Rwanda in 1994. They were killed in approximately one hundred days by their fellow countrymen, the Hutus, in one of the most devastating mass exterminations of this century.

According to Philip Gourevitch's heartbreaking book, *We Wish to Inform You That Tomorrow We Will Be Killed with Our Families: Stories from Rwanda* (New York: Farrar, Straus and Giroux, 1998), there was no United States–Bill Clinton–Madeleine Albright–United Nations–NATO intervention in the genocide of these African people.

In fact, the Clinton administration's ambassador to the UN, Madeleine Albright, opposed leaving even the skeleton crew of two hundred seventy

[UN troops] in Rwanda. Albright went on to become Secretary of State, largely because of her reputation as a "daughter of Munich," a Czech refugee from Nazism with no tolerance for appeasement and with a taste for projecting U.S. force abroad to bring rogue dictators and criminal states to heel. Her name is rarely associated with Rwanda, but ducking and pressuring others to duck, as the death toll leapt from thousands to tens of thousands to hundreds of thousands, was the absolute low point in her career as a stateswoman. (pages 150–1)

One of the most poignant (and almost funny were it not so horrific) moments in Gourevitch's book is when the author describes a hotel manager, Paul Rusesabagina—who became a hero in the resistance against genocide in Rwanda— surrounded by the *genocidaires* (Hutu killers) outside his hotel, sending faxes to "Bill Clinton himself at the White House" (page 132).

PAGES 108–110 *"bleeding from the head":* From "Police Arrest Co-Worker in Slaying of Woman" by Ron Sullivan, *New York Times,* June 23, 1992:

According to police, Ms. Steinberg entered the store [the Gap] with the manager at 8:15 a.m. . . . When the manager returned a few minutes before 10 a.m., he found Ms. Steinberg bleeding from the head and neck wounds near an open safe. . . . Twenty-year-old Anwar Abdul, former maintenance worker at a mid-Manhattan Gap store, stands accused of killing the twenty-two-year-old assistant manager. . . . Mr. Morgenthau said Mr. Abdul stabbed Ms. Steinberg in the neck, then took about $3,500 from the opened safe and escaped unnoticed.